CW00485241

Cockerels and Vultures
Poems of the First World War

Cockerels and Vultures
Poems of the First World War

ALBERT-PAUL GRANIER

Translated by Ian Higgins

Saxon Books

Cockerels and Vultures

ISBN 978-0-9528969-7-5

Published by Saxon Books, Bishops Close, Hurst, West Sussex BN6 9XU
UK

Website: www.warpoetry.co.uk

Printed and bound in Great Britain by 4Edge Ltd, 7a Eldon Way,
Eldon Way Industrial Estate, Hockley, Essex SS5 4AD UK

First printing October 2013

Second printing January 2014

Third printing July 2014

Copyright

Selection, translation into English, introduction and notes –
copyright © Ian Higgins 2013.

Ian Higgins (as translator) asserts the moral right to be identified as the
author of this work in accordance with the UK Copyright, Designs and
Patents Act 1988.

All rights reserved. No part of this publication may be reproduced, stored
in a retrieval system, or transmitted, in any form or by any means,
electronic, mechanical, photocopying, recording or otherwise, without the
prior permission of the translator in writing. He may be contacted directly,
but in the case of difficulty, application may be made to the publisher.

Cover photograph

The cover photograph is the last known photograph of Albert-Paul Granier,
Second Lieutenant, 116th Heavy Artillery Regiment, 1917.

Cover photograph copyright © Paul Granier Estate, Copyright 2013. Used
by permission.

Contents

Foreword

Albert-Paul Granier's unique poems speak for themselves, whether in French or in English. However, even in France, he was until recently completely unknown except to a handful of surviving relatives. A brief account of his life and the rediscovery of his work will help those interested to situate his poetry historically and culturally.

Albert-Paul Granier – I shall call him Paul from now on, because that is how his family refer to him – was born in 1888, in Le Croisic, on the Atlantic coast of Brittany. He grew up in an atmosphere of high culture, classical and contemporary. Writers, painters and musicians, among them Gabriel Fauré, were frequent visitors to the house. Paul himself was an amateur composer and an accomplished pianist as well as a poet. Tall and well built, he was also a keen sportsman, playing football, tennis and rugby, and riding, boxing and fencing.

In 1908, after passing his Baccalauréat in Latin, modern languages and philosophy, Paul went to the University of Nantes, where he read law and was president of the Students' Union. He qualified as a solicitor in 1910, the ultimate aim being to join his father's legal practice. First, however, he had to do his three years' compulsory national service. He therefore spent the years 1911–13 as a trainee artillery officer at the officer cadets' training college of Saint-Cyr, just outside Paris. The proximity to Paris meant that there were plenty of concerts to go to, an experience which has left its mark on some of the most striking poems in the present book. Paul was also able to join a group of poets who met to read their work to one another. Among these poets were Gabriel Fauré's son, Philippe Fauré-Frémiet and, according to one source, Paul Fort and Émile Verhaeren.

Less than twelve months after he completed his national service, war broke out, in August 1914. Paul was mobilised straight away, serving mostly in the Verdun region, but also on the Somme. He was mentioned in dispatches, praised for his coolness and courage under fire and his efficiency in liaison between artillery and infantry. In December 1916, he volunteered for training as an airborne artillery observer – a grisly way of realising his long-cherished ambition to fly. Meanwhile, in the midst of all the horror, he was writing the poems of *Les Coqs et les Vautours* (*Cockerels and Vultures*). Published in Paris in 1917, the book was singled out for recommendation by the Académie Française in 1918. But Paul Granier did not live to enjoy this honour: on 17 August 1917, over the battlefield of Verdun, a shell – reportedly French – smashed into his aircraft. His body was never found.

And that was that. Apart from three poems and a short entry by Fauret-Frémiet in Volume 3 of the huge *Anthologie des écrivains morts à la guerre* published by Malfère in 1924–26, Paul Granier disappeared completely from any but local Breton memory.

Then, in May 2008, at a jumble sale in the little Breton town of Mesquer, a passing poet, François de Cornière, spotted a slim volume lying on the ground between two stalls. Naturally, he picked it up. It turned out to be *Les Coqs et les Vautours*, a book he had never heard of, by a poet he had never heard of. Reading the poems, Cornière was bowled over. He gave the book to the novelist and journalist Claude Duneton who, equally astonished, persuaded the Éditions des Équateurs to publish the text in October 2008. Since then, *Les Coqs et les Vautours* has created quite a stir, prompting comparisons especially with Guillaume Apollinaire, still the only one most people in France will think of if you ask them to name a Great War French poet. In truth, while Granier is Apollinaire's equal as a war poet, his is a completely different voice – different, indeed, from that of any of the other major French poets of the war (and there are many such, whatever your French friends may say). Similarly, in terms of subject matter and emotional impact, he readily bears comparison with any of the canonic British poets of the Great War, but he has a completely individual way of seeing and expressing the war.

It would be needlessly coy not to complement the story of Paul Granier's rediscovery with some picturesque home-grown detail. In 1987, I had the good fortune to be asked by Tim Cross, organiser of The Armistice Festival of 1988 and editor of the accompanying transnational anthology, *The Lost Voices of World War I*, to oversee most of the French section of the anthology. In the end, we included eighteen Belgian and French writers, some well known, some less known – and one totally unknown, save for the three poems in the Malfère volume and Fauré-Frémiet's invaluable few words . . . A measure of this obscurity is that, of all the 59 writers included in *The Lost Voices*, Paul Granier was the only one for whom we could not find a photograph or portrait.

Although there was only space for four poems, printed with the French texts and my translations side-by-side, Granier was, for both Tim and me, *the* great discovery of the whole enterprise – so much so that, a few years later, I returned to the Bibliothèque Nationale in Paris and copied out the rest of the collection by hand (the librarians quite rightly being unwilling to photocopy more than a few pages of the volume, given the fragility of its paper). Back in Britain, I typed it up, and have since shown it to French-speaking friends, some of them students of French poetry. While acknowledging the occasional echoes of Laforgue and Verhaeren, they have all commented on the originality of this poetry ("It's like Surrealism, only it makes sense", said one), the inventive musicality and rhythms, the expressive unorthodoxy of the punctuation, the paradoxical child-like vulnerability and gritty toughness of a generous mind attempting to encompass and express the unimagined new sorts of nightmare that the war was flinging at ordinary people day by day.

These reactions gradually led me to dream of translating the whole collection and sharing with the English-speaking public the surprise and admiration with which François de Cornière, Claude Duneton, Tim Cross and many others have first encountered these poems. I am therefore very grateful to Saxon Books for enabling me to turn this dream into a reality. I am grateful, too, to Elspeth Christie, David Gascoigne, Esther Higgins, Walter Shillito, Nigel Wilkins and Martin Gibson, principal timpanist of the Royal Scottish National Orchestra, for their help and advice. Finally, I owe warm and heartfelt thanks to Paul Granier's nieces, Françoise Granier and Solange Granier-Nobécourt, and, above all, to his great-nephew, Jérôme Nobécourt, for their unstinting encouragement and material help: without their support, this book would not have been what it is.

Ian Higgins

Albert-Paul Granier, 1888–1917

. . . And so then, for all in time of war, here
are the cockerels, clamouring defiance,
and the vultures, ponderous with hate,
talons stained with the blood of memories . . .

Hate

O gentle fellow dreamers,
how fondly do you charm the dreams,
how skilfully ride the will o' the wisp;
how your peaceable heroic souls
thrill to breathe among the galaxies . . .
— O you devoted lovers of the stars, we have now
to turn our backs on the spellbinding sight
of dreams dancing shimmering into magic flight,
the roomfuls of calm and well-wishing,
the still inwardness of reflections in their mirrors,
the ministering lamp's caress of gold . . .
Ah, those soft, silent, lampglow evenings
coaxing the play of sheen and sparkle,
like a woman looking at jewels,
from the gleam of verse white-cushioned in its book;
the fevered nights, drunk on thought,
intent over poems
as gem-cutters over stones . . .
— All that! We have to leave it all behind!
We, the nectar-gatherers of the mind, have now

to grasp that old, long-wearied longbow of the will,
and flex and tense it
and let fly Hatred, stinging shafts of Hate!

Hate! Hate! How the word hurts!
Hate, we have to hate!
Hatred unto ecstasy.

1914

The Drums

The deep-rolling growl of the drums
comes rumbling closer like thunder
and hail beating time on slate roofs;
the avalanching growl grows, grows,
spreads and unfurls in billows of rhythm,
like roaring blood around the roads,
great arteries of highroad.

Blood? The blood is coming,
in the rhythm of the drums . . .
From the hearts of people everywhere —
city people, village people,
plains people, forest people,
mountain people, seashore people . . .

Deep-rolling its thunder, the growl
comes up to the crossroads
and a scattery troop of chattering children
skip to meet it with shrieks of delight.

Bucking and bumping on powerful thighs, the drums
pound past, the growl a raging cyclone now;
there's a thunder, a throb, and every chest in unison
resounds to the bellowing thrum:

and you can hear, in your own listening heart,
at this crossroads,
the heart of the Nation thudding in the drums.

1914

Exodus

To Émile Verhaeren

Away along the claggy tracks
leading in from the plains,
the people are leaving, gone mad perhaps,
gone wisely mad perhaps,
the people are going — away, anywhere but here . . .

Into long carts done out with hay
they've loaded their worldly wealth:
their Sunday best,
mattresses, white blankets,
the photographs of the boys
away in the war,
and the grandmother's bridal spray
in its glass dome,

                    and they go away,
leaving Christ above the hearth,
that His supplicating arms might turn aside
the brutal looting rampage of the soldiery:

An aged horse, gaunt on poverty,
led by a child,
hauls a trap, panting,
with women and an old man
following on foot, not to weary further
the broken-down old horse's weary tramp —
following the trap
like the hearse of their past,
following in resignation,
dragging their cattle,
those neat pointed feet and gentle eyes . . .

The people are leaving, people
who long were mad perhaps,
and staring now
at visions only they can see:
memories perhaps, or hopes . . .

From village to village,
wordless, starving, pinched,
away the people drag — some
dropping where they trudge, dead meat already —
their only future — when not death —
the fields in flames and the farm looted,
— away, to bury their hate like dead cattle,
bunch their knuckles to their eyes,

slump down and weep on a heap of stones,
choke weeping . . .

Away along the claggy tracks
leading in from the plains,
the people are leaving, gone mad perhaps . . .

Les Éparges. August 1914

Sunday

The bells ring hesitantly through the rain;
ring; timidly ring,
distantly calling
after those who have gone, vanished
into misty distances . . .

The little church, grieving, grey,
no bigger than a chapel,
the little church
kneels amongst its dead,
timidly, dolefully calling
for whoever will bring consolation.

Clusters of soldiers, down
from the haylofts and barns,
haggard men in muddy coats,
stream slowly up
towards the patch of land
where the church keeps vigil for its dead.

The little church is startled
to have so big a congregation back;
startled — and glad,
and in a sudden burst of sunshine
its windows are sprinkled blue and gold,
like a smile from the heart
through the tears of rain.

Between the limewashed walls,
with their Stations of the Cross
in naive paintings, centuries old,
the soldiers have squeezed in,
packed into uniform rows,
and all the vibrant youthful voices
are singing canticles and psalms
from long ago.

The old church is glad —
never has it had so big a congregation,
nor ever did its frail spire
reverberate to such a choir.

And, thrilling to every verse,
all those soldiers' souls
from all around in the vaulted air gather
and together beam their own bright light
towards the sun-in-splendour monstrance —

And the little church is glad to hear again,
through the whispering murmur of the rain,
the bells sing out their full refrain.

September 1914

Squall

A steel squall of gluttonous thrusting shells smashed
thunderclaps through clear sky
straight at the village, ferocious
as a swoop of eagles on a flock of grazing sheep.

And when the bloated eddies of smoke had rolled away
across the quiet pastureland,
the peaceful village by its river
was gone, and in its place was only ruin, desolation.

The church, amidst the dead of years past, is doomed,
but just still standing, like a dying horse, its very soul
bleeding from the riven stones,

weeping from every dead louvre in the lurching belfry
that it cannot sound this night a pious death-knell
for the peaceful village by the river.

1914

War Song

Dame Death is joyously dancing,
a drunken, hip-swinging jig,
never a word, just wriggling
and playfully juggling skulls
like so many knucklebones.

Dame Death is glad, and very drunk —
for there's blood in full flow out there,
a heavy red brookful in every ravine.

Accompanying her weird dancing
is the tom-tom of guns in the distance:
 "Tom-tom-tom! tom-tom-tom! Come then, White Lady,
come dance to the sound of the drums!"

Dame Death's getting drunker and splashing
her sweet little face with blood,
like a child who's been eating the jam.

Dame Death is paddling in blood,
and slapping down into it with her long hands,
as though she were washing her shroud;
wallowing, and silently sniggering.

Dame Death is flushed, writhing, dancing
like a girl who's had too much drink.

"Hey, Death, get your hopping in time
with the tom-tom of guns in the distance!"

— Tomtomtom-tomtomtom!
              The guns in the distance
quicken their murderous presto,
guns laughing together in rhythm;
the guns in the band force the tempo,
whipping her up for The Jubilation Ball:

"Spin on those dainty thin heels,
squirm the meat off those sinuous hips,
get waltzing and whirling, White Lady!
dancing and skipping! waving your arms!
Here's blood, here's blood!
And here's some more, to keep you busy!
Come on now, drink up! totter and reel!
This is the start of the Orgy in Red!"

Dame Death is dancing, insanely drunk,
to the tom-tom of guns in the distance.

1914

The Fort

In commemoration of Fort Troyon

This small fort, thickly ridged in a caparison
of stubby humps and terraced parapets,
hunches and flattens among the grasses,
hunches and flattens, like a wary mastiff.

The fort crouches, watchful,
tensing by the livid ponds,
like a jungle cat ready to spring.

The fort has squat, blunt turrets,
like big bulbous eyes
scouring the horizons, scouring
the distance where what will be will be . . .
and on its back
each black gun points a muzzle,
each great gun a Cyclops,
unblinking, staring —
at what? and where? —
out there, somewhere out there . . .
staring at someone still unseen,

but who could appear one day
from behind a skyline twilight-red with burning
and come surging in a stench of murderous butchery
with fat fistfuls of lightning,
someone shall come from beyond,
ignore the frontier signs and come
with ravening hounds of thunder,
from somewhere out there . . .

And on that day, through its arteries
of tunnels and corridors and galleries
men shall stream like blood,
live blood, vibrant blood,
and pour through damp, dark pits
down to hell, and bring back up
from where volcanoes suck their molten lava
death-seed encased in iron eggs.

The Stranger, the Alien, shall say: "Silence, fortlet!
Snarling won't help you —
it's one thousand of us, to one of you!
Just let me through, and keep your hatred to yourself!
One hundred thousand of us, to one of you!"

And in that torrent of horror the fort shall bristle,
grind the thousand teeth of sliding grates and grilles
and, growling like a loyal watchdog,

gnash the air in the savage jaws
of its hundred suddenly unmuzzled guns
and hurl through space, across whole valleys,
their seed of death —
Dear mothers! — Seed,
of death.

And soon the truculent fort,
hacked and gouged by iron into fearsome gashes,
its steel voice suddenly shrapnel-choked,
shall cough a final gunflash,
and then, through its breached walls, bleed heroic blood,
all that blood made of men, suddenly
coagulating, clotting into corpses,
bleed that fine proud blood out into the countryside.

The fort, brooding death deep underground, waits:
the fort, crouching among the acacias,
waiting in its fur of branches and leaves,
waiting, watching the horizons,
watching for someone still unseen . . .

1914

Bivouac

Ten of them there are, all round the fire,
ten men watching in a silent circle,
never tiring of the skittish fire
dancing to amuse them.

The fire wriggles and flounces
and wrestles itself into knots,
then flings back out and cavorts
like an acrobatic clown
in shimmering incarnadine silk,
and gurns and chuckles to cheer them up,
juggling sparks,
endlessly cutting tricky new capers —
then, all at once, it starts a different game.

The fire gives a twirl, then scales the logs
like a cock on a dunghill:
The fire chatters and chirps, prattling away
as the men intently listen:
It speaks to them of long winter evenings
with harsh winds that catch and tear on the roofs;
of the goodly warmth from a fireplace
the size of a theatre;

it speaks of the tales that Granddad always tells
of sailing away to far-off islands,
and the magic stories
that Granny barely more than whispers
to the wide-eyed little ones;
it speaks of the good old dog, pensively
sitting by the flickering hearth,
and the cat curled up purring on a knee;
it speaks of hopes of going home one day,
and joyous victory songs
and drinking songs
round a festive table,

and the fire speaks of love . . .

*

Round the fire, the men
reach out towards the flames
to catch a hold of the swirling dreams,
bright mirrors of their souls —
but the fire leaps up and pirouettes,
and cackles, and starts its daft antics again . . .

. . . and the visions are gone, with the smoke . . .

November 1914

Troops

One homogeneous mass of undulating,
monstrous, multiple movement,
the powerful creeping roadful of troops
is an intensity of will, intent
on endless slow advance,
towards horizons of rout
where Death the Huntsman, in full array,
tots up his bag for the day.

Along the road, towards the sun,
moves the slow, endless crawl of troops,
splattering red glints
and a rattle of scales.

The men march on,
brows burning with one Idea,
jaws jutting with one grim Will;
the men,
chewing on their fierce hatred, march on
to find out whether, at the horizon,
Death the unrelenting has finally relented . . .

And behind them, like a faithful dog,
steals shadow,
black shadow,
impalpable, implacable —
behind each one of them
a soft, lithe shadow, twisting, darting,
with never a sound,
like cats in alleys.

Slyly, step by step, each shadow
creeps, fluid, flat to the ground,
lest its man look round
and see it:

If he sits down, it curls into a ball;
if he lies down, it creeps under his body —
always there, alert, and patient,
waiting for Death's order
to spring at Man and seize him,
and voraciously gnaw him into atoms
and then, slowly, scatter the crumbs
across the desert of Space . . .

Onward march the troops,
stubbornly, tenaciously;
slowly, step by step, the troops
undulate their way towards their Destiny;

and they know that behind them
slink shadows, watching, waiting —
but give them no attention.

Onward march the troops
in fierce, calm intent,
following their shining one Idea,
troops on the march, heedless
of the shadows behind them
like a horde of wolves.

— Watch out, men! Watch out!
Death's uncoupled
his most ferocious pack of shadows!
Death's let loose his legendary pack
of war hounds!

Watch out, men! Watch out!

1914

The Mortars

Juddering iron buckets clanging,
jerking deadweight chains clanking,
the thunderlumbering caravan
labours on, along the baking roads and tracks,
all thunderous crash and clash.

The straining, weary horses
ponderingly nod,
as though to doubt
their onward slog will ever end . . .

Wheels as thick as millstones
mill the crunching road.
And in towns and villages along the way
thunderstruck groups watch
the deadweight cortege of death grind past,
the squat carriages, bolt-stubbled muscles bulging,
and, mute, menacing, brutal,
the black barrels, muzzled and bound like lunatics.

1914

Night

Along the bony, and wrinkled, and rough
and crevassed and fractured road,
the heavy black convoy of guns
clumps and jerks and lumbers,
all clanks of jolting steel and clinking rifles,
splashing its clatter all over
the sleepy echoes in wayside ponds.

In the darkness
a wind, whistling softly through its teeth . . .

Behind the wagons, the ludicrous lamps
swinging in men's hands
set shadows hopping from the huge wheels
as the flinty highroad skins them.

Then, suddenly, a rider turns in his saddle
and shouts "The Town!"
                       Along where the road bends,
two gaslights dim with doubt
give a flutter, as though in hope:

jabbing spurs claw at hot flanks,
and the horses force their weary muscles,
steaming in the evening chill.

"The Town!"
                    Up ahead
the flickering gaslights watch us and wait,
red crests ruffling in the evening wind,
inquisitively wondering
what monstrous convoy can be so slowly dragging
along these roads through the muffled night . . .

The heavy wagons in procession
launch their avalanche roar
between the neat white houses
and walls and empty courts:
now and then, a straining horse skids
and the cobbles shift and ring
to the iron scrambling of its hooves.

It's late, and the windows are shut,
and the lights are out, and all's at rest,
and only the inquisitive gaslights
watch in silence as the mighty caravan
hobbles and clunks past.

But, in one empty little square,
two shutters, just two, have blinked apart,

like somebody dreaming . . .
and glowing on the ceiling
is a hazy golden halo
from a lamp, under its shade
of tinted crystal.

What atmosphere, what delicate serenity
that crystal dome creates:
oh, to be there, in that silence
so giving of ideal and reflection;
to be there listening to the lamp's whispering,
gentle and affectionate, like a lover's;
to be up there, with the whole town asleep,
and dream dreams of things unknown, unformed,
and watch the wispy whirls of dream
in that haloing caress of light
easing the dark . . .

But the caravan has blundered on,
hypnotised by its atrocious purpose,
trampling the silence with steel,
with never a thought
for the empty square, or the little lamp
under its green crystal dome,
gently cradling someone's dreams,

and along the bony, and wrinkled, and rough
and crevassed and fractured road,

the heavy black convoy of guns
has clumped and jerked and lumbered
through the night, on its ferocious pilgrimage,
splashing its clamour all over
the echoes asleep in wayside ponds.

1915

Obsession

The guns go rolling on their way,
the crushing wheels mill the road,
the guns roll on towards a dawn
dissolved in the night,
like blood in stagnant water.

Fantastical, an exodus of steel!
The killing machines roll on along the road,
one by one,
and every one the same,
like some apocalyptic travelling zoo
wandering towards the Gate of Hell,
wandering, horizon by horizon,
looming abruptly over valleys
brimful of concrete dark,
and rolling on, crunching and creaking
towards uncertain dawns . . .

Obsession, these endless journeys,
in the night;
Obsession, nightmare,
these processions of vague shapes

that might be lugging wagonloads
of blocks of night to wall in the Dawn,
or something sinister
like corpses of executed men:

Obsession,
intense obsession,
this obstinate, nervous trek between soft ditches
where throngs of inexplicable dark shadows
crouch in quintessential black Shadow
and shriek the silence . . .

Obsession,
acute, obsessive obsession,
this relentless onwardness,
with sometimes the sudden fear
that like Lenore's phantom horse
my own might all at once, without a sound,
vanish from under me,
and the savage caravan of steel machines
dissolve into the dawn . . .

Searing, piercing,
hallucinatory
Obsession.

September 1914

The Battle

Since first light, coiled in the dew,
they'd been baying, turn and turn about,
a raucous hawking, out through fretful space;

baying Death, out through fretful space;

rearing their black necks like snakes striking,
spewing hatred by the mouthful,
as we stoked the blaze of their ferocity
and heard the air rasp in their steel jaws

and the echoes slammed about the hazy distance —
thunder, rolling, growling, giant thunder
like a Titan hefting an anvil
and hammering on the bronze door of heaven.

But vaguely, too, somewhere far off
was the baleful voice of enemy guns
bellowing hatred of its own through the vastness,
and the heavy shells hooting overhead,

since first light,
and now night slyly building in the distance.

Out round the slaty horizons
serried echelons of echoes rumbled,
and bursting shells were meteors
puncturing the looming dark.

Suddenly, the distant fierce growl was still,
leaving just our great panting guns to roar
and put to flight, away from those horizons
into the dense night, the enemy guns
hobbling slowly off like wounded toads;

and in all their weary pride
they proclaimed their victory to all the Universe,
and stamped the ground in madcap triumph,
for the mighty far-horizon voice was still,
and only echoes answered, like muffled drums.

So then, in the night,
with nothing left at which
to spit the shellfuls of hate and terror,
they stopped for breath;

but, with the silence back,
I stole out, between the tents, alone,
and lovingly, gently,
with this puny hand,
I patted those weary guns . . .

Souilly. 1914

The Horse

There was once a fine great warhorse,
a handsome horse with a golden coat.

Head held high, mane
a banner flowing in the wind,
he would arch his neck, scan the skyline,
cock his tawny ears, alert,
and when fanfares blared
and guns blasted,
spring like a catapult released
into the cataract of noise,
nostrils tensed, scenting conquest,
and his whinny, like a fierce trumpet call,
proclaimed his joy at coming triumphs.

But the days went by, day after day,
and fatigue bit into his flesh,
and pulled and tore at those splendid muscles,
and one day his weary rider
took off the bridle and the saddle,
and after one last loving pat
turned and left him there,

and walked away,
and not once looked back . . .

And there the great horse stands,
weary of head, limp of ear, dull of eye,
at the roadside, on his own,
in the overgrown grass,
too feeble even to recall
the red of recent battle,
stands there,
limp and listless, on his own,
like a dead man still on his feet.

This was once a fine great warhorse.

1914

Nocturne

Night spreads calm, soothes the desolation.

Searchlights prospect, reaching over with their livid arms,
probe vague wasteland space, assessing void and expanse,
dissect, inspect, with fingertip precision.

In plush ravines, unravelling in horror
and ravenously chewed at by the shells' sharp teeth,
lie pallid corpses, clinging fast, with their rigid fists,
to the Nothingness kneeling darkly by.

The anxious wounded tauten every thought
towards that misty elsewhere of things lost;

burned-out villages are embers glimmering through the night,

and devoutly, gently, her smile shimmering through her grief,
good sister moon, O pale eternal,
veils the dead in shrouds of opal.

1914

The Kill

Into the wet autumnal forest, where sound
trembles like clear droplets at the tips of twigs,
into the yellowing forest
fragrant with the balm of silence
I walked, alone, this September morning,
through thickets quick with silken tremors,
to drink the calm and the serenity,
to drain the heady solitude
and grant my soul the blessing of a moment's peace.

Among the trunks and the banks of arching branches
I looked — I confess,
gently drawing leaves aside
like a child who spots a nest, I looked —
to see if there were not some nymph asleep
amongst her billowing golden hair;
but times have wearied of such sunny legends,
the suns of times long gone have died,
and all I chanced upon, against a bushy elm,
was one small violet, in the silky moss,
one frail wandering stray from departed spring.

The silence was as troubled as a perjured soul,
a silence like a pond tormented by the rain,
a silence weeping for the vanished days of kings a-hunting . . .

Those horns, muffled by the calm, the distant horns,
the horns, the horns October calls forth
together with the grieving bells of All Saints' Day
and its wreaths of wet chrysanthemums —
the horns no longer sound their languid echoes
along the mossy, wet forest tracks,
and the echoes of the weary bells
bustle and fade among the russet leaves.

Suddenly, the branches juddered;
the guns' long jaws clamoured out a harsh fanfare,
like somebody bashing a drum in.

It's a kill, a kill, this autumn's kill,
the kill, the kill of men at bay
the tromboning catapulting guns are blaring —
one, and then another, and another, and another,
through the evening calm,
trajectories like tentacles
thrown high across the forest, their suckers
the shells insatiably draining distant lives . . .

The horizons echoed for a while,
juggling bits of blast around,
then lost interest;
and calm returned
to the dreaming forest
of the hunts of legend,
a strange, desolate calm,
the specious tranquillity
of a graveyard, or a desert . . .

'Tis a kill, a kill, this autumn's Kill!

Verdun. Bois des Fosses, 1914

Back to Base

Black guns, rolling through the sepia night,
very slowly, very heavy, very weary,
very slowly rolling to the slow plod
of six horses plumed with moon;

Very heavily, the black guns
are lumbering back to their den,
lumbering — and a bit unsteady,
with all the cordite they've sunk —
lumbering in single file along the road,
very slowly . . .

The wheels are hard oak, and grate and creak,
and hiss like angry snakes,
and whimper with hate — and
with longing, to buck and rear again
back there in the forest clearings.

Thirsty horses, hungry men,
great black guns drunk on glory
rolling home in the night,
to line up and then not stir till morning,
sleeping off their victory.

From dawn to dusk they strained
their sleek necks and shoulders,
avalanching steel at tangled mist,
goring tusk-thrusts at the golden forest,
hurling invective over the horizon.

They've fractured, hacked and killed a whole army;
walls are down, roads ploughed up;
the foreign guns, with all their fancy ratchets
and clever engineering, are wrecked, lying
overturned on top of torn corpses:

the scything steel wind they've been blowing
has reaped the corn for sovereign Death.

The panting horses bunch their rippling muscles,
strike stripes of sparks along the dim road.

The six guns roll on, almost in reluctance:
the six guns roll on through the black night,
weary, but so proud in victory,
voluptuaries of pride and power and triumph,
like oriental monarchs raised by Death
to godhead, in their eternal, fateful dark;

and now and then, briefly, a horse's shoe
sows a row of germinating stars . . .

Verdun. 1914

Wildfire

Down into the barn
a shell came crashing,
like the hopes of all the years collapsing,

and from the shell, jack
from tiny box, sprang the devil fire.

Through the great slatted door
I see fire rise and sneak
among the season's gathered straw and hay,
then, chattering in glee,
dance in sparks across the floor
a light fantastic reel . . .

Fire knows it has the run of the place,
and prospecting, paces out its new demesne,
climbs the beams and eaves,
then slides back down on the heaps of straw
like a haymaking child left to play.

Fire skips and whistles with glee,
ripples, flows, unfolds and spreads,

and punches window-panes
to take a peep outside:
Fire mellows wormy timbers
with velvet crimson,
splits open sacks of grain
and spills cascades of gold and ruby,
then bushes up between the tiles
and red-heads the roof;

Fire nuzzles through the slats to look,
and strokes the wood, illuminating every fret
with gaudy scarlet.

Fire's cutting loose in glee;
there's no one now to spoil its sport
and torment it with the hose
it used to seethe to,
big cat to the tamer's whip.
Fire dances whooping through the blazing barn.

Then, when it's had enough
rumbustious ladder-tumbling,
it swarms unruffled-burglar-like
up over the roof, breaks the tiles and
like a child in a tantrum
who suddenly takes against his game,
twists off the breaking door,

punches in the roof and brings it down,
and jumps onto the house behind:

Inquisitively, through the skylights,
it looks inside, snake-necks about inside,
and suddenly it's itching
to poke and pry and play again,
and dance itself breathless,
like a drunk in a pub . . .

Fire, monster of beauty,
beautiful, unstrokeable,
pacing the village
like a tiger in its cage . . .

Keur-la-Grande. 1914

The Church Tower

The old church tower, shroud-bound in rolling fog,
is now a catafalque of solitude,
silently weeping, this bleak evening,
for the voices of the silent bells . . .

Last year's calls to prayer are long gone,
wandering lost in forest clearings.

The old tower, grey in the grey murk,
stands in the burnt-out village
imploring from dilapidated space
echoes of those calls to prayer,
lost and gone into thin air . . .

All Saints, All Saints,
Day of remembrance of the dead:
the old tower so wants
once more to tell its dead they are remembered,
and softly touch the graveside flowers
with the Miserere's gentle wing;
the old tower stands distraught,
like a mute so wanting to speak,

and silently weeps for its silence,
and weeps for the shell-split roofs below
gaping like demented skulls . . .

The old tower feels a dull despair
at this excruciating solitude,
and begins to dream
that perhaps at any moment
the fatal shell will rip down through its timbers,
and like some fearsome sexton
ring the mad, collapsing, bounding bells
in celebration of remembrance,
for all who ever died here in the village
since time immemorial . . .

The old church tower invokes the gun,
calls forth the distant savage shell
to ring that last, that final knell.

The bells?
      . . . Perhaps they've simply flown out,
invisibly riding the air
as though to welcome the Spring,
and after their long silence
their voices will peal out and sing
the hymn of Deliverance,
the magnificent Resurrection —

And the little village, like one
who has come close to dying,
will rejoice to hear its heart suddenly beating
in the bells, in the old church tower.

All Saints' Day, 1914

Poor Dogs

Round the pitiful villages,
round the burnt-out hamlets,
the dogs, the poor bewildered dogs, go mutely padding
to and fro among the shell-holes,
searching for the doorstep,
searching through the scattered rubble
and collapsed roofs,
stepping over charred beams,
sniffing uncertain scents.

The poor dogs' friendly eyes,
innocent and gentle,
implore the soldiers:
"Tell me, please tell me,
where's the rough and ready master,
the kindly mistress,
the little children who played with me?"
— those friendly amber eyes, questioning,
innocent and gentle . . .

The poor lost dogs pad soundlessly like shadows
to and fro in villages of rubble,
like memories in madmen's heads.

1915

The Cathedral

Guns, old comrades!
old slumberers suddenly roused
from long, deep fortress-sleep,
ancestral steel black-muscle-bound,
heavy veterans, barrel-jawed,
connoisseurs of cordite,
steel-eaters, fire-smokers,
proud, full-throated singers —
sing out the lovely wedding hymn
of pale mankind and death!
Sing it! Sing! Sing again!
let the echo thunder from inside
every resounding cloud
to repeat the mighty funeral chorus,
the fearsome, red-lightning-candled
wedding march.

Growl, my old friends, clamour, turn
and massacre, annihilate!
They have assassinated the Cathedral!
— smashed the high doors down,
smashed the stately legends

of the saints tall in their stained glass,
and the golden light and purple shade
of the prodigious rose window,
that symbolic radiant monstrance
illuminating an ecstatic world!

They've blasted the high arches in,
smashed down the colonnades of pinnacles
that hungered for the sky,
slashed to shreds the lacework of stone,
killed the silence that had forever slept
under solemn vaulting . . .

*

O guns, good guns, my old friends!
over all the endless plains
clamour forth the universal pain!
The Cathedral that transcends humanity
is dying; howl death,
like roaming dogs in moonlight,
shout! roar! Louder, ever louder!
roar open-jawed, roar my hatred at them!
Avenge the gentle stained-glass saints
who for centuries shone down
in stately absolution,

avenge the wingless angels
and the grey lead gargoyles
smelted in the flames!

They have assassinated the Cathedral!

O guns, good guns, my guns,
my poor voice is shouted hoarse!
shout for me, roar for me
your most colossal execration,
hurl my anathema, my curses,
cry vengeance! cry vengeance!
and I shall feed you all the lovely cordite
and heavy steel that you can swallow!
rear and stamp, like maddened horses!
spew cataracts of hate on them!
Roar! roar! even unto death!
and roar your dying gasp!
O guns, good guns, my friends!
they have murdered memory!
they have
assassinated the Cathedral!

1914

Music

Snow was filling space with a dream of down . . .

At the crossroads, the fountain was frozen . . .

And as I was walking
past the stricken water,
over my snow-blank soul
there stole delicate light harmonies,
fluid through the mothy whiteness,
like echoes of harmonicas,
harmonies of the aether,
like whispering cherubim,
like a miracle of angel strings.

By the crossroads, in a barn,
a man,
cheek gently leaning to the violin,
was stroking melody from gut
with the taut, white bow.

This was marvellous music,
exquisite in slenderness and grace,

with runs, arpeggios and double-stopping,
breathing its soul among the snow
— the dry, white snow —
in shimmering rainbows of shot silk:
That music wrapped me round in dream,
a halo of enchantment,
full flower of fulfilment,
as if I could see, beyond vision,
a lovely sylph with hands of snow
juggling with pearls,
crystals and precious stones,
or an iridescent sequined fish
lured from fable,
with glistening
prismatic skin
scattering impalpable
diamond-splashes through the air . . .

Cataclysmic guns
smashed from somewhere
through the evening,
like hurricanes colliding.

The slow, persuasive, sleepy snow
was a soothing gentleness
to the percussive, panic-stricken leap of echoes,
and the marvellous music

resumed its fragile paradigm of watered light,
a swaying weave of ecstasy,
like a luminous fountain,
and so frail, on the wavering crystal of its stem . . .

And I stood there, in the quiet snow,
like a child
listening to stories on Christmas Eve.

Rupt-devant-Saint-Mihiel. 1914

Searchlights

Glancing long, methodical, blue,
the searchlights coolly feel among the clouds —
searchlights turning
dazzle-moustached blue snouts
to stare unblinking,
following some invisible thing,
signalling to the planets.

The lights project their astral calm
up into the aether,
as if the search were for some lost comet
veering out of orbit,
frantic in the void . . .

Their phosphorescence opens blue pathways
in the cloud, like those
the angels in old frescoes follow down
into a valley to gather souls.

The lights look desperately zenithwards,
great dilated pupils endlessly peering
in the dark . . .

The searchlights are insane with fear,
they break through the night like a mirror,

and sink in empty quicksand space . . .

1915

The Volunteers

Iron-clad in ice, the road
is scrabbled at and gripped by shod hooves
as the cart slowly lumbers away,
sprouting soldiers and tangles of waving arms:
the cart setting off, who knows where to . . .
off somewhere, at a slow walk,
who knows what for . . .

tousled with shouts and laughter.

The cart is fizzing with intensity,
whirling all its voices into clouds
as it lumbers away, dishevelled with sounds
like a railway train mushroomed with smoke.

The voices swirl and settle
on those left behind, standing at the roadside;
the voices fade away, like the pink steam
round huddles of tidy trackside shrubs
along the platform in country stations
when there's no noise from the trains . . .

The cart, glittering with glints of metal,
swarming with tingles of energy and hope,
rumbles calmly on, towards victory,
or disaster and rout,
to the slow, hard tread of its eight horses.

January 1915

The Balloon

The grey balloon floats down to the forest horizon,
the balloon floats down, like some planet of doom,
orbit completed,
sinking into the sea.

The grey balloon, heavy with inquisitive treachery,
slips imperceptibly beneath the trees.

And the white birches that shield me,
— such slender stems, martyred in their prime —
the birches, born on the soil of France,
bundled and dumped like faggots
along with hornbeam and oak,
the white birches ruffle their feathery bark
into hackles of anger.

Observation post. 1915

Dusk

Night pillows the valley with mystery
where the aching river
strangely floats —
a pale scrap of bruised sky
torn off by sudden raging shells
and fallen slowly down from space
into the valley, its grave.

A long shred of twilight sky lies
in the valley, dying,
the grey poplars keeping vigil
like standing monks;

and the stars, slowly pulsing into prayer,
so pale in all the bloodying of the dusk,
compassion blinking in their glistening eyes,
mourn the sky shredded by those raging shells,
the torn, dead sky
the mist is burying.

Observation post, Meuse. 1915

Nocturne

The guns have fallen silent, gagged with fog,
in the winter's night that cancels space,
and a calm, full of menace
as the screech of owls over castle walls,
hangs in the many-hearted silence.

Sentries, peering out,
tense every muscle, edgily
awaiting the unexpected.

A thwack like wet cloth
sounds from the valley —
sudden muffled rifle-shots
unsure of guessed-at shadows
and the rustling emptiness.

Tonight
is like the nights in Breton legend
when hell-hag washerwomen
kneel invisible at riverside stones,
beating shrouds in the thick water.

Observation post, Meuse. 1915

The Andante . . .

The rain, endlessly unravelling;
the rain, shovelling at the mud the whole sullen day;
the rain, unendingly sobbing its toneless chords;
and the whispering wind, crumbling the cloud into drizzle . . .

Why, this evening, am I haunted so
by that majestic Andante
from the Seventh Symphony?
Its chords, as magnificently simple
as the triumphal arches of the ancients,
hold me in a vast enchantment.

Its harmony is velvet to my soul,
its murmur a caress that soothes
the melancholy as we pick our way
along the bank of this canal.

The rain has never stopped . . .

The mud is all long, snaking rivulets of agate
and clouded onyx, chopped into splashes
with every drawn-out hoof-fall of my horse.

The rain has never stopped, the whole lead-blue day.

The Andante
gently eases my resentment
with its divine serenity . . .

Ah, those Sundays, not two years ago —
the Sunday afternoons, the lamp-lit hall,
the huge orchestra a single mind and spirit
in every flying bow-tip:
The miraculous fluid
a fountain spreading up to the galleries, then
falling like snowflakes onto souls laid bare,
like springtime sunlight through stained glass
on a girl's communion veil.

The Andante,
the Andante is gentle, with a touch of sadness,
like an autumn evening over ponds,
or the voix céleste of an organ;
and my chrysalid soul
weaves itself a wonderful cocoon
from this aching blessedness,

on the purple silk weft of the rain.

On the road to Chauvoncourt. 1915

Autumn

The horizons are adrift,
iridescent long processions
of horizons drifting off in waving mists,
away into the grey;
a blurring, fluid drift.

Bleary Autumn, flanked by poplars,
silently floats along the slow canal,
like the pilgrim prince of some dead city —
a Memphis, or a Thebes — leaving,
to the cadence of the oars,
on board his quinquereme
with beautiful slave girls and rarest silks.

Autumn, carrying away its treasures of light
along the unruffled water,
Autumn is slowly emigrating,
like all those people, just a year past,
who set out across the plains
with all their belongings in children's prams.

For this is an invasion —
Winter's invaded, Winter's coming;
the sky did fight back with thunderstorms,
but is leaving now, resigned and silent,
while, like little girls in their white dresses
for Corpus Christi, the tall poplars
softly shake their branches
and shed their golden leaves.

Troyon. 1915

Spleen

My soul, this evening, inclines to tenderness;
my soul is misty, gossamer-fine,
in slantwise drift, like grey drizzle —
because of a book I've been reading,
a tender, gently melancholy book,
with talk of love . . .

. . . love . . .

This tender inclination of my soul
is like a hillside gently levelling out,
lowering its pine groves to the plain;
impressions barely brush against me, light and soft,
like soap bubbles on wool,
bobbling shimmers of magic colour.

*

My heart is like a wild cat,
suspicious, savage, scared;
my heart has vicious claws, and teeth —
but it's scared, scared of Future,

Future in the seethe and ferment of cities,
civilised Future . . .

My wild heart is scared, it's shivering,
it's forgotten how to speak of love, forgotten
how to snuggle softly up
against a woman's heart;
my heart, my wild heart —
where is the woman would tame it?

May 1915

The Fire

The fire, in its hearth,
has that soft, supple sound
of oriflammes and blue pennons
in procession through a fishing port
for the ritual quayside blessing of the sea.

The fire very softly
crackles the dry branches,
and they sag, and crumple, with a silky crunch
like a rustling skirt or footsteps in snow.

The flames stretch
from the tangle of twigs,
reaching up towards the light,
like human souls . . .
— reaching for the clear light
up beyond the chimney,
unravelling towards the light,
like weed in the current . . .

Chattancourt. 1916

Nocturne

In the treacherous, million-mysteried night,
vague presences are sensed,
numberless in the clammy, spongy night —
soundless; there; intense:

The forest is instinct with energies
that lurk behind each bush:
they lurk, they watch . . . they loom,
like the very soul of darkness.

Ghostly fingers prod at the distant skies,
then more softly prowl the heights.
Split-second fen-fires gigantically ignite,
and the stillness of the glades is rent,
as though with gathering witches devil-sent,
by the werewolf howl of shells in flight.

In the forest. April 1915

Song to the Moon

"Moon, O mistress mine, O moon,
make haste, come out from there!
The attack's tonight — it's imminent!
Why are you there, among the trees?
Why there, behind their lines?
Have they made you prisoner
and got you on a tether, like a fat balloon
dangling a man?

"Moon, fair mistress moon,
hurry, out from there —
down here in the trench, believe us,
we love you so, you know we do,
and you know it would grieve us
if the guns were to hurt you!"

And the moon laughs, among the black treetops;
and the moon mocks, among the white rockets
jostling like fireflies
round her white face.

"O mistress ours, we Pierrot clowns,
we beg you, please be quick,

we clowns are worried sick —
you're up just where the shells will fly,
and laughing, and we can't see why!

"'Two o'clock,' the General said —
and so, at two, the dance shall start!
Moon, O mocking moon,
sniggering, obstinate moon,
mock not! — oh yes, you'd look swell
with a ten-inch shell
full in your face!

"H-hour! God almighty! — Here they come,
all the shells, all hurtling up,
all flinging towards you,
a pack of wolves, a tourbillion
of lunatic shells by the million!
— O moon, sweet mistress mine,
your graceful white loveliness be spared!

"God almighty! — Moon, suddenly
your head's all bloody! Oh hell,
those are fifteen-eights
gone up and punched your face!
O moon, poor moon, O moon,
are your looks gone for good,
and so soon?

Such grief on the ground!
— At least find a scrap of cloud
and bandage your wound!

"Moon, O moon, poor moon!
we pale Pierrots of the trench,
would we Pierrots were safe abed —
O graceful moon, O lovely moon,
what tears we Pierrots are going to shed!"

Attack at Vermandovillers. August 1916

The Attack

To Captain Grillet

"You there, behind the parapet,
what are you men doing?"

    "Sir, Spring's coming, Sir:
birds darting among the branches,
only, this year
they're so quick you can't see them —
and these birds buzz, like bees!"

    "Sir, take cover, Sir,
why don't you take cover?"

      "What a racket!
                  Ah, the bastards —
bullet through my water bottle, and it was full!"
     "And that gas is parching!"
     "Too bad, I'll eat snow —
what's left between the shell-holes
and isn't poisoned . . ."

Steel is mattocking the white earth,
turning it over in blasts of smoke;

82

the earth erupts like rockets through the branches
and falls back, black, on the snow,
gesticulating roots.

Evening thunderstorms in cities,
fat raindrops on glass canopies,
loud, splatting raindrops,
gale-force nights at sea,
high waves against the cliffs:
this evening, these are all become steel hatred —
this ferocious, nightmare evening.

The steel squeals in the seething air,
chiselling fluted columns of noise
with shell-bursts for capitals:
The steel's fierce mattocking goes on
in a frenzy of splinters
that hackles up the flesh of the trees.

The air is gritty with explosions,
then smoothed by the cool flight of the Austrian shells,
like a musical caress,
a caress of oboes and fifes,
with the pizzicato bass continuo
of heavy mortars in the distance,
as the eighteen-pounders blare
and the five-nine timps give the orchestra a beat.

"Whop! Wham! — Sir,
we're not in time;
Whop! Wham! the dance is whipping up:
whoever is it dances to this —
Death?"

"Whop! Wham! Timpanist, you're insane —
don't thump your skins so hard,
timpanist, you're nowhere near in tune!
Come on, tune up, give those keys a twist!
Here, the thunder'll give you an A!"

"Whop! Wham! The timpanist's insane!"
"What? Still no contact?
None of the runners back,
and no one any idea
what that machine-gun's jabbering at?"

"Right. Time to say goodbye, Sir."
"Coming with me, lad?
Good man, thanks.

Well, let's go!"

"Whop! Wham! What a lovely symphony —
is it Dukas, d'Indy, d'Udadidynkiki???"
"But the orchestra really are insane —

not one of them's keeping time
and the timpani's not in tune!"

Whop! Wham! The orchestra's insane!
And wielding the baton is Death.

Verdun (Bois des Fosses. Bois d'Hardaumont).
21–24 February 1916

The Ravine

Down the great ravine, to the rock-hacked floor,
where the sluggish gas snags and poisonously hangs,
the mighty field gun blundered and plunged, clanging,
tolling; rolling like a corpse into its hole.

The six crazed horses sheared their traces, crashed
through the shattered scree that every shell-burst
thunders in and echoes and the echoes bounce
and surge in a whirling tidal smash . . .

And in the dark ravine, the great black gun
there lies — agape, alone, straining in vain
its upturned muscular wheels up at the thundering,

unmoved at the snapping, biting shrapnel,
unmoving, mute, like some great dead raptor
still jabbing its talons up at its conqueror.

Ravin de Beaumont. Bois des Fosses.
22 February 1916

Fever

"Heartbeat, heartbeat, why the rush?
Whither the headlong dash,
where are you taking me,
where is this punishing mad gallop
dragging my dishevelled life?"

My heart is racing off, up through the clouds,
over the mountains, across the plains —
not Pécopin himself, on Satan's thoroughbred,
flew as swift through all those haunted years
as me, on this runaway heart
careering like a wild stallion.

　　"Where are you rushing me, heart?"
　　"To a white hospital, in a quiet garden,
women softly rustling through the wards,
and, at nightfall, distant tranquil bells
murmuring a call to evensong;
to a white hospital, and a peaceful death,
a woman's white hand on your pale brow,
and precious words of comfort on her lips."

"No, rampaging heart! No!"

"Fetch my horse!"
— Sooner the fierce alarm-cry of guns
announcing torrents of thunder-strikes;
and sooner than the nurses' soft footsteps,
give me merciless flying splintered steel
whizzing invisible just above our heads!

No, heart . . .
                    Let me die beside rearing guns,
in the mad triumph of this great Epic,
die lying here, in the mud and the blood,
my eyes filled with sky, my heart with stars,
here, soothed by the moon's affectionate caress,
with a great chunk of steel in my chest!

1916

War

Ahoy there, boys! Mariners ahoy! —
War
is as fierce as a storm-force gale at sea,
war is as murderous, raw, ferocious
as the equinoctial ocean
shrieking with wrecked ships on reefs in the night;
war, all of a sudden dead calm;
war demented, savage, merciless —
war is gorgeous, boys, I tell you!
war's as gorgeous as the sea . . .

The trench is a petrified wave,
a wave alert and silent,
boiling-over pent-up power
— your power, boys!
— the trench is a tidal wave unsheathed
that suddenly erupts in slashing spray and spume and fumes,
a hurricane of sheer noise.

The bullets yowl like spindrift;
in the panic-stricken wind, winged torpedoes

abruptly tilt and dive,
like gulls into foam.

Further out, the invisible,
cataracting, shattering shells
slam at blockhouse steel,
implacable as raging breakers,
and burst in sudden sprays of blossom,
great bouquets of hissing smoke,
like some fantastical riptide
butting at the cliffs.

And overhead, the multiple trajectile roar,
like the one and undivided clamour of the sea.

1916

Notes on the Poems: Some Echoes and Allusions

Exodus

This poem is in some ways reminiscent of the work of its dedicatee, the Belgian poet Émile Verhaeren (1855–1916), whose evocations of the "hallucinatory" impact of rapid industrialisation and urban growth on the demoralised countryside had won him international fame by the early twentieth century. There is some evidence that Granier had met Verhaeren while doing his national service at Saint-Cyr.

The Fort

Fort Troyon was a small fort on the Meuse, about 18km south-southeast of Verdun, with a garrison of 450. It was constructed of stone, and covered with a six-metre-deep layer of earth. In September 1914, a division of the German Fifth Army crossed the Meuse further south, and the fort was all that prevented it from encircling the city. After a heavy bombardment on 8th September, a German delegation went up to the fort and demanded its surrender. The French commandant refused, and the bombardment, alternating with infantry assaults, resumed on 9th September, pausing on the 13th and then continuing for several days later in the month. The fort sustained massive damage, but was never taken. Verdun was not encircled and, arguably, German forces in the decisive Battle of the Marne (9th–15th September) were crucially weakened by the inability of a whole division of the Fifth Army to join them.

The Mortars

Dated 1914, this poem well conveys the tension and foreboding widely felt at the outbreak of the war. However, just before this book went to press, I was shown a newly unearthed manuscript of the poem, on which it is stated that it was written on the occasion of a major military exercise in 1912 – that is, while Granier was doing his national service. With one striking exception, there are only a few small differences between the manuscript and the published text; Granier had clearly found his characteristic poetic voice. But the exception is perhaps a telling one. After "Wheels as thick as millstones/ mill the crunching road", the manuscript has seven lines which have been left out of the final text and which roughly translate as follows:

> And, mouldy with grey dust,
>
> men follow, heavily, dejectedly,
>
> as if bearing to its burial
>
> the coffin of their youth,
>
> and wearily they watch,
>
> mile by dragging mile, the future to come
>
> Coming.

Do these line express resentment at wasting three years playing at soldiers? Or do they show an awareness – unusually shrewd for the time – of what modern warfare will turn out to be? At all events, there is in these lines a sullen despair which would have been at odds with the tough-minded resignation of the rest of *Cockerels and Vultures* and would, in any case, very likely have been cut by the censor before publication in 1917.

Obsession

In *Lenore* (1773), by Gottfried August Bürger, Death, posing as Lenore's sweetheart, whisks her off on a nightmarish ride through the night. At cock-crow, Death reveals himself, a skeleton with scythe and hour-glass, and Lenore's horse sinks and vanishes beneath her. The poem was a major influence on the development of Romanticism in Europe. Gérard de Nerval produced several French translations of it, the first in 1830.

The Cathedral

Rheims Cathedral is a Gothic masterpiece with many unique architectural features, including angels with spread wings. It was where French kings were crowned. It sustained serious damage from German artillery in the first two months of the war, particularly on 20 September. In one bombardment, roof timbers caught fire and the lead on the roofs melted, pouring down through the gargoyles. Pictures of the semi-ruined cathedral were used by French propaganda throughout the war as examples of "German philistinism and barbarity".

The Andante . . .

Whose seventh symphony? We can rule out Haydn and Mozart. Dvořák's Seventh was still known as the Second in Granier's day. Schubert's was not performed in orchestral form until the 1930s, Schubert himself never having fully orchestrated it. Mahler's was only composed in 1905, so is unlikely to be referred to as "the" seventh symphony. Brückner's is a remote possibility, but it has no andante movement. Neither, unfortunately, has Beethoven's — yet the whole atmosphere of the poem suggests the second movement of this symphony. It is actually marked allegretto, but is more often than not played andante, sometimes even adagio. It is virtually certainly the only one of these symphonies that a reader in 1915 would even have heard of, let alone heard in performance. So let us assume that "the Seventh Symphony" is Beethoven's.

Song to the Moon

The readiness with which Granier coins new words in *Les Coqs et les Vautours*, especially in making verbs out of nouns, is sometimes reminiscent of the poetry of Jules Laforgue (1860–87). This poem contains no such coinages, but there are unmistakable echoes both of Laforgue and of the Belgian Symbolist Albert Giraud (1860–1929) in its hint of nihilism, its unsettling mixture of attitudes and registers, its parodic veneration of the Moon, its adoption of the maudlin, absurd pierrot persona and its comic rhymes (cf. Laforgue's *L'Imitation de Notre Dame la lune* and Giraud's *Pierrot lunaire*, the latter set to music by Schoenberg in 1912).

The Attack

The poem is dated 21–24 February 1916. Assuming that it was written in the immediate aftermath of the attack described, there is a grim dramatic irony for the French reader in 1917: Granier could not know that 21 February was the first day of what was to be the Battle of Verdun, a bloodletting which lasted until December. Both the Bois des Fosses and the Bois d'Hardaumont were taken by the Germans in the first week. According to Étienne Port (in *Le Fureteur breton*, Nov.–Déc. 1919), who had taught Granier at primary school and remained in touch with him to the end, the soldier who volunteered to go with Captain Grillet was Granier himself.

Fever

Pécopin is the protagonist in Victor Hugo's *Légende du beau Pécopin et de la belle Bauldour* (1842), a florid tale in the style of Rhenish legends, translated into English in 1902 as *The Story of the Bold Pécopin*. The week before he is to wed his adored Bauldour, Pécopin is tempted to join a magnificent hunting party. One thing leads to another, and he ranges the earth for five years until, despairing of seeing Bauldour again, he meets a nobleman who promises to take him to her the next day, if he will only spend this night hunting with him. The nobleman is in fact the Devil, whom Pécopin had unwittingly lamed and disfigured in a previous encounter. The ensuing "frantic, vertiginous, supernatural gallop" carries him off from Europe to the Tropics to the Arctic, before bringing him, as promised, to Bauldour's castle. Alas, the night has lasted a hundred years, and Pécopin, who has not aged, does not recognise Bauldour, a hideous crone of 120 . . .

Ian Higgins

The Translator

Ian Higgins has published widely on French poetry of the two World Wars and on translation. Among his translations are *Chagall's World* by André Verdet (The Dial Press), *Piranesi* by Pierre Seghers (Forest Books), *Jacques Rozenberg, a Tribute: Painting and Thought* (Andrée Caillet-Rozenberg), *Florilegium*, texts by Francis Ponge with engravings by Jane Kennelly (Epsilon), prose and verse by nine writers in *The Lost Voices of World War I*, edited by Tim Cross (Bloomsbury), and thirteen poems by French writers in *We Are the Dead – Poems and Paintings of the Great War, 1914–1918*, edited by David Roberts (Red Horse Press).

Since the dramatic rediscovery of Albert-Paul Granier in France, in 2008, Ian Higgins has been in close contact with the poet's surviving relatives, and is uniquely placed to introduce this remarkable writer to English-speaking readers.

Ian Higgins lives in Fife, never far from the "one and undivided clamour of the sea" that echoes through Granier's poems.

Also published by Saxon Books

Minds at War
Poetry and Experience of the First World War
Edited by David Roberts

This groundbreaking anthology of First World War poetry will appeal to people who wish to encounter both key poets and poems but also read more widely and gain a deeper understanding of both the poetry and the mindsets of people caught up in the First World War. It includes the great classic poems of the war, poems by many women poets, and unfamiliar poems that enjoyed huge popularity at the time they were written, all set in an historical context, with many revealing insights from diaries, personal letters and accounts, pronouncements by the media, politicians and others. This volume  includes contemporary photographs and cartoons, maps, biographies, glossary and bibliography. *Minds at War* is an illuminating, fascinating, moving and comprehensive anthology of First World War poetry. It is widely used in academic institutions in Britain and America.

410 pages   9"x 6"   Paperback   Illustrated
Eighth printing   ISBN 978-0-9528969-0-6   £15-99 UK

Out in the Dark
Poetry of the First World War, in Context and with Basic Notes
Edited by David Roberts

 This 192-page anthology contains the most important poems and poets of the First World War, but there are also many other poets of special interest, with women poets particularly well represented. The most celebrated poets – including Wilfred Owen, Siegfried Sassoon and Isaac Rosenberg – have been given whole chapters. Their work has been arranged in date order so that the development of their ideas and techniques may be appreciated. Comments of past and present day critics, and basic explanatory notes on unusual expressions and vocabulary make this poignant anthology especially valuable for students. Extracts from poets' diaries and letters, historical and biographical notes, fascinating photographs and drawings give further insights into the lives, experience and thinking of the war poets.

192 pages   9"x 6"   Paperback   Illustrated
Ninth printing   ISBN 978-0-9528969-1-3   £10-99 UK

For more information visit www.warpoetry.co.uk